C000135092

Now yo[u]
clarinet soloist on eight specially
recorded arrangements

Classical
COLLECTION

TAKE
THE
LEAD

clarinet

IMP

International MUSIC Publications

International Music Publications Limited
Griffin House 161 Hammersmith Road London W6 8BS England

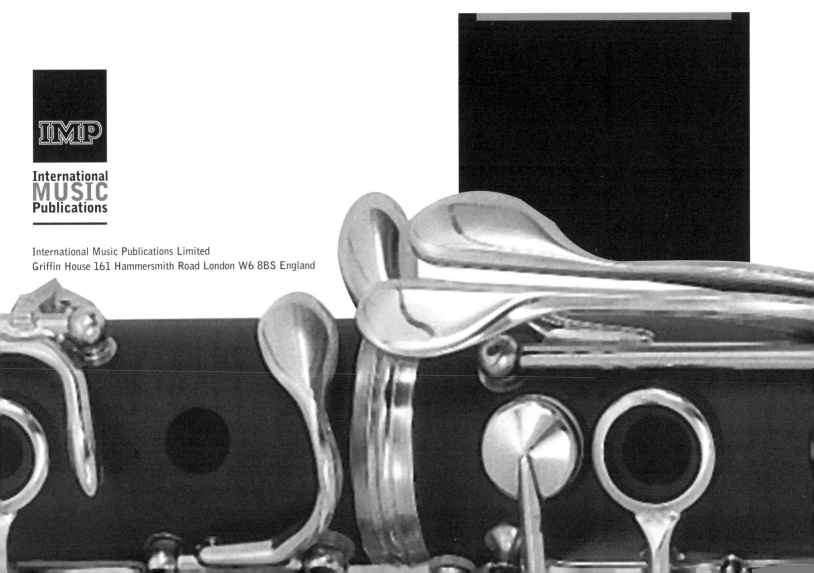

Series Editor: Anna Joyce

Editorial, production and recording: Artemis Music Limited
Design and production: Space DPS Limited

Published 2000

International MUSIC Publications

© International Music Publications Limited
Griffin House 161 Hammersmith Road London W6 8BS England

Exclusive Distributors:

International Music Publications Limited

England:	Griffin House 161 Hammersmith Road London W6 8BS
Germany:	Marstallstr. 8 D-80539 München
Denmark:	Danmusik Vognmagergade 7 DK1120 Copenhagen K

Italy:	Nuova Carisch Srl Via Campania 12 20098 San Giuliano Milanese Milano
Spain:	Nueva Carisch España Magallanes 25 28015 Madrid
France:	Carisch Musicom 25 Rue d'Hauteville 75010 Paris

WARNER BROS. PUBLICATIONS U.S. INC.

USA:	15800 N.W. 48th Avenue Miami, Florida 33014

Australia:	3 Talavera Road North Ryde New South Wales 2113
Scandinavia:	P.O. Box 533 Vendevägen 85 B S-182 15 Danderyd Sweden

clarinet

TAKE THE LEAD

In the Book...

On the CD...

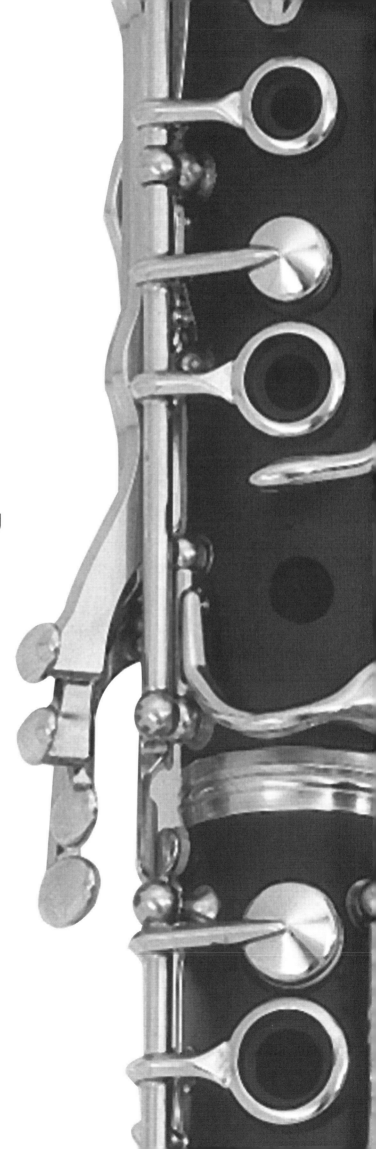

Demonstration   Backing

Dance Of
The Sugar Plum Fairy

(from *The Nutcracker*)

Music by Peter Ilyich Tchaikovsky

Demonstration   Backing

Radetzky March

Music by Johann Strauss Snr

In The Hall
Of The Mountain King

(from *Peer Gynt*)

Music by Edvard Grieg

12

accel. al fine

Demonstration   Backing

Polovtsian Dance

(from *Prince Igor*)

Music by Alexander Borodin

Demonstration

Backing

Sheep May Safely Graze

Music by Johann Sebastian Bach

Demonstration

Backing

Symphony No.40
in G minor, 1st movement

Music by Wolfgang Amadeus Mozart

Molto allegro

Demonstration Backing

The Swan

(from *Carnival of the Animals*)

Music by Camille Saint-Säens

Demonstration

Backing

The Toreador's Song

(from *Carmen*)

Music by Georges Bizet

You can be the featured soloist with
TAKE THE LEAD

Collect these titles, each with demonstration and full backing tracks on CD.

90s Hits

The Air That I Breathe (Simply Red)
Angels (Robbie Williams)
How Do I Live (LeAnn Rimes)
I Don't Want To Miss A Thing (Aerosmith)
I'll Be There For You (The Rembrandts)
My Heart Will Go On (Celine Dion)
Something About The Way
You Look Tonight (Elton John)
Frozen (Madonna)

Order ref: 6725A – Flute
Order ref: 6726A – Clarinet
Order ref: 6727A – Alto Saxophone
Order ref: 6728A – Violin

Movie Hits

Because You Loved Me (Up Close And Personal)
Blue Monday (The Wedding Singer)
(Everything I Do)
I Do It For You (Robin Hood: Prince Of Thieves)
I Don't Want To Miss A Thing (Armageddon)
I Will Always Love You (The Bodyguard)
Star Wars (Main Title) (Star Wars)
The Wind Beneath My Wings (Beaches)
You Can Leave Your Hat On (The Full Monty)

Order ref: 6908A – Flute
Order ref: 6909A – Clarinet
Order ref: 6910A – Alto Saxophone
Order ref: 6911A –Tenor Saxophone
Order ref: 6912A – Violin

TV Themes

Coronation Street
I'll Be There For You (theme from *Friends*)
Match Of The Day
(Meet) The Flintstones
Men Behaving Badly
Peak Practice
The Simpsons
The X-Files

Order ref: 7003A – Flute
Order ref: 7004A – Clarinet
Order ref: 7005A – Alto Saxophone
Order ref: 7006A – Violin

Christmas Songs

The Christmas Song
(Chestnuts Roasting On An Open Fire)
Frosty The Snowman
Have Yourself A Merry Little Christmas
Little Donkey
Rudolph The Red-Nosed Reindeer
Santa Claus Is Comin' To Town
Sleigh Ride
Winter Wonderland

Order ref: 7022A – Flute
Order ref: 7023A – Clarinet
Order ref: 7024A – Alto Saxophone
Order ref: 7025A – Violin
Order ref: 7026A – Piano
Order ref: 7027A – Drums

The Blues Brothers

She Caught The Katy And Left Me A
Mule To Ride
Gimme Some Lovin'
Shake A Tail Feather
Everybody Needs Somebody To Love
The Old Landmark
Think
Minnie The Moocher
Sweet Home Chicago

Order ref: 7079A - Flute
Order ref: 7080A - Clarinet
Order ref: 7081A - Alto Saxophone
Order ref: 7082A - Tenor Saxophone
Order ref: 7083A - Trumpet
Order ref: 7084A - Violin

Latin

Bailamos
Cherry Pink And
Apple Blossom White
Guantanamera
La Bamba
La Isla Bonita
Livin' La Vida Loca
Oye Mi Canto (Hear My Voice)
Soul Limbo

Order ref: 7259A - Flute
Order ref: 7260A - Clarinet
Order ref: 7261A - Alto Saxophone
Order ref: 7364A - Piano
Order ref: 7262A - Trumpet
Order ref: 7263A - Violin

Jazz

Birdland
Desafinado
Don't Get Around Much Anymore
Fascinating Rhythm
Misty
My Funny Valentine
One O'Clock Jump
Summertime

Order ref: 7124A - Flute
Order ref: 7173A - Clarinet
Order ref: 7174A - Alto Saxophone
Order ref: 7175A - Tenor Saxophone
Order ref: 7179A - Drums
Order ref: 7178A - Piano
Order ref: 7176A - Trumpet
Order ref: 7177A - Violin

Swing

Chattanooga Choo Choo
Choo Choo Ch'Boogie
I've Got A Gal In Kalamazoo
In The Mood
It Don't Mean A Thing
(If It Ain't Got That Swing)
Jersey Bounce
Pennsylvania 6-5000
A String Of Pearls

Order ref: 7235A - Flute
Order ref: 7236A - Clarinet
Order ref: 7237A - Alto Saxophone
Order ref: 7238A - Tenor Saxophone
Order ref: 7239A - Trumpet
Order ref: 7240A - Violin